I0421897

The Story of a Special Day
Volume 79

March 19

78th day of the year
(79th in leap years)
287 days remaining
until the end of the year.

by Michael Dobson

Timespinner
Press

March 19: The Story of a Special Day (Vol. 79) is copyright © and trademarked ™ 2013 by Timespinner Press. All rights reserved. The Timespinner Press logo is trademarked by Timespinner Press. This book is also available in ebook form for Kindle, epub devices, and other formats from your favorite online booksellers.

For more information about the series, about me, or about your special day, please email us at editor@timespinnerpress.com.

Look for other volumes in *The Story of a Special Day*, coming often.

Table of Contents

March 19 Quotations.. 2

Event of the Day 4

March 19 Holidays and Celebrations........................... 8

What Happened on March 19?..................................... 11

Who Was Born on March 19?...................................... 22

Who Died on March 19?... 55

March: The Third Month 68

March Symbols 69

March Events 70

March Zodiac Signs 75

What Day of the Week is March 19? 77

Copyright, Credit, and Contact 79

Cover: War Bonds poster featuring a Tuskegee Airman, for the Event of the Day.

Back Cover: The month of March, from the French Gothic illuminated manuscript *Les Très Riches Heures du duc de Berry.*

March 19 Quotations

"In a gun fight, you need to take your time in a hurry."

— Wyatt Earp, born March 19, 1948

"Of the gladdest moments in human life, methinks is the departure upon a distant journey to unknown lands."

— Sir Richard Francis Burton, born March 19, 1821

"I cannot and do not live in the world of discretion, not as a writer, anyway. I would prefer to, I assure you — it would make life easier. But discretion is, unfortunately, not for novelists."

— Philip Roth, born March 19, 1933

"They say you shouldn't say nothin' about the dead unless it's good. He's dead. Good!"

— "Moms" Mabley, born March 19, 1894

"I wasn't so interested in being paid. I wanted to be heard. That's why I'm broke."

— Ornette Coleman, born March 19, 1930

"Many people consider the things government does for them to be social progress but they regard the things government does for others as socialism."

— *Chief Justice Earl Warren, born March 19, 1891*

"Destiny is not a matter of chance; it is a matter of choice. It is not a thing to be waited for; it is a thing to be achieved."

— *William Jennings Bryan, born March 19, 1860*

"The attitude that nature is chaotic and that the artist puts order into it is a very absurd point of view, I think. All that we can do for is to put some order in ourselves."

— *Willem de Kooning, died March 19, 1997*

"Biography should be written by an acute enemy."

— *Arthur Balfour, died March 19, 1930*

"Clarke's First Law: When a distinguished but elderly scientist states that something is possible, he is almost certainly right. When he states that something is impossible, he is very probably wrong."

— *Arthur C. Clarke, died March 19, 2008*

"Businesses owned by responsible and organized merchants shall eventually surpass those owned by wealthy rulers."

— *Ibn Khaldun, died March 19, 1406*

Tuskegee Airmen Activated

Captain Andrew D. Turner, Tuskegee Airman

The role of African-Americans in the U.S. military is tangled up in the long history of slavery and racial discrimination. In the American Revolution, black soldiers served in northern militias but generally not in the South. Blacks were forbidden to serve in the Marine Corps until 1942, but permitted in the Navy from the beginning. The Army forbade black enlistment until the beginnings of the Civil War.

The Buffalo Soldiers, African-American units that fought in the Indian Wars, filled six cavalry regiments. Officers, however, were usually white. Eighteen members of the Buffalo Soldiers earned the Medal of Honor. In World War I, over 350,000 black soldiers saw service in Europe, where such units as the 369th Infantry "Harlem Hellfighters" achieved distinction.

In the Second World War, many black units were relegated to support, but still won acclaim, as in the case of the Red Ball Express that supplied Allied units in France. The 761st Tank Battalion "Black Panthers" was commended by General George Patton.

African-Americans were not permitted to become military aviators until pressure from the NAACP and other groups led to the formation of a black Army Air Force unit. Initial flight training for black aviators took place in a segregated facility in Tuskegee, Alabama, from which came the name by which they are best known, the Tuskegee Airmen. Unlike most black units, the Tuskegee Airmen also had black officers.

The first unit of Tuskegee Airmen, the 99th Pursuit Squadron, was activated on March 19, 1941. It was assigned to a white fighter group serving in North Africa and Sicily. The group commander told reporters that the unit was a failure and that its pilots were cowards, resulting in Congressional hearings to see if the program should continue. The squadron's black commander, Col. Benjamin O. Davis, later the first African-American general in the U.S. Air Force, argued forcefully and publicly for his men, and the program continued.

There was to be a black bomber unit as well, the 447th Bombardment Group. It was commanded by a white officer who was an avowed supporter of segregation, and the group never saw active service. Three additional fighter squadrons were trained, and together formed the 332nd Fighter Group, also commanded by Davis, now promoted to full colonel.

The 332nd was stationed at Ramitelli Airfield on the Adriatic coast of Italy. It escorted heavy bombers of the 15th Air Force on bombing raids, and also performed dive-bombing and strafing missions. The unit initially flew P-40 Warhawks before receiving the P-51 Mustangs with which they are most identified.

Bomber crews nicknamed the Tuskegee Airmen "Red Tails," or sometimes "Red-Tail Angels," from the distinctive red tail markings on their aircraft. The Germans called them *Schwarze Vogelmenschen*, or "Black Birdmen."

The Tuskegee Airmen achieved a remarkable combat record. The 332nd received the first of three Distinguished Unit Citation for a mission against a tank factory in Berlin, shooting down several Me-262 jet fighters. Individual pilots earned 1,000 awards and decorations, including a Silver Star and 96 Distinguished Flying Crosses. Of the 992 pilots in the program, 150 lost their lives. The claim that no bomber escorted by the Tuskegee Airmen was ever lost to enemy fire turns out, however, to be false. However, the average number of bombers lost on Red Tail-escorted raids was about half what other fighter units of the 15th Air Force achieved.

After the war, many Tuskegee Airmen went on to great distinction, especially after President Truman's 1948 desegregation of the armed forces allowed them to serve in previously all-white units. Three Tuskegee Airmen (including Davis) made flag rank: General Daniel "Chappie" James, Jr., became the first African-American four-star general. George Lucas's 2012 movie *Red Tails* provides a film portrayal of the unit, and many other films, TV shows, and documentaries chronicle them as well. From postage stamps to statues to Congressional gold medals, many honors have been given to these brave pilots.

March 19 Holidays and Celebrations

Minna Canth's Day (Finland)

Minna Canth's Day is the day of social equality in Finland. Minna Canth (March 19, 1844 — May 12, 1897) was a Finnish writer and social activist. She is the first woman to have received her own flag day in Finland, beginning in 2007.

Saint Joseph's Day (Western Christianity)

Saint Joseph of Nazareth, husband of Mary and guardian of Jesus, has his feast on March 19 in Western Christianity. (Eastern Christianity celebrates his day on the Sunday after the Nativity.) Because March 19 falls during Lent, St. Joseph's Day feasts usually contain only meatless dishes.

In Italy, Saint Joseph's Day is an occasion to give food to the poor. People often wear red clothing and eat a Sicilian pastry known as zeppola. In Malta, people typically go to Mass in the morning and picnic in the afternoon.

In the Philippines, an old man, a young lady, and a small boy, chosen from the poor, are dressed as St. Joseph, Mary, and Jesus, and are given a feast.

In New Orleans, people build private and public altars to St. Joseph and distribute food to the poor. There is a tradition that burying a small statue of St. Joseph upside down in your front yard will make your house sell more promptly.

The week prior to St. Joseph's Day in Valencia, Spain, is celebrated as *Las Fallas*. People prepare giant puppets or dolls, known as *ninots*, that often satirize people. The week is celebrated with fireworks, traditional dress, and parties. On the final night, the ninots, which are carried on foundations known as *falles*, are burned.

Father's Day (Spain, Portugal, Belgium, Italy, Honduras, and Bolivia)

Father's Day in these countries is held on the same day as Saint Joseph's Day, honoring all fathers who care for their children.

Return of the Swallows (Mission San Juan Capistrano, California)

The American Cliff Swallow (*Petrochelidon pyrrhonota*) migrates each year between Argentina and the American Southwest. The return of the

swallows to Capistrano is traditionally celebrated on
Saint Joseph's Day, and the swallows depart again on
Saint John's Day, October 23. Today, fewer and
fewer swallows return to Capistrano because
development has reduced their habitat.

Unity Day (Kashubian region of Poland)

The Kashubian ethnic group is located in Eastern
Pomerania, a region in northwestern Poland.
Kashubians are a West Slavic people of Pomeranian
origin who speak Kashubian, which is sometimes
classified as a language and sometimes as a Polish
dialect. The city of Kartuzy, near Gdansk, is their
traditional capital. Unity Day celebrates Kashubian
traditions and history.

Quinquatria (Ancient Rome)

The Roman festival of Quinquatria was March 19 in
honor of Minerva, goddess of poetry, medicine,
wisdom, and commerce. Women would consult
fortune-tellers and the temple of Minerva would be
ritually purified. In the year 59 CE, the emperor
Nero used the occasion of Quinquatria to try to
assassinate his mother Agrippina.

What Happened on March 19?

The abbreviation "O.S." on some dates refers to the fact that the Russian Empire did not switch from the Julian to the Gregorian calendar at the same time as the rest of Europe, and therefore some figures have two dates for their birth or death.

People whose original names are not in the Western alphabet have their native names in the appropriate script shown in parenthesis.

1279 CE – Battle of Yamen (厓門戰役)

The Naval Battle of Mount Ya, March 19, 1279, is a contender for the status of the largest naval battle in history. It was the last stand of the Chinese Song Dynasty against invading Mongols. Although the Mongol forces had only 50 warships, against a defensive force of over 1,000 mostly non-combatant ships, the battle ended in crushing defeat for the Song forces. At least 100,000 died in the battle, filling the surface of the sea with bodies, including the body of the eight-year old boy emperor Bing of Song (宋帝昺), last of his line.

1861 CE - First Taranaki War Begins

The First Taranaki War, fought between the indigenous Māori people and the British government of New Zealand, ended on March 19, 1861, about a year after it began. Over 3,500 British troops from New Zealand and Australia fought against a Māori force of up to 1,500. The war ended in an inconclusive ceasefire, setting up further land wars between the British settlers and the Māori, which today are fought in courtrooms rather than on the battlefield.

1863 CE – Sinking of the *CSS Georgiana*

The ironclad Confederate steamer *CSS Georgiana* was to be the most powerful cruiser in the Confederate Navy. Built secretly in Scotland, she was caught by Union blockaders outside Charleston, South Carolina on the night of March 16, 1863. The *Georgiana* tried to flee, but to no avail, and was crippled by gunfire. The Confederate captain signaled his surrender, but instead scuttled his own ship nearly a mile off shore, and escaped on the ship's boats with all his men. The wreck was found again on March 19, 1965, but the reputed 350 pounds of gold it was supposed to be carrying have never been found.

1865 CE – Battle of Bentonville

The American Civil War Battle of Bentonville took place from March 19 to 21, 1865, in Bentonville, North Carolina, the last battle between Union General William Tecumseh Sherman and Confederate General Joseph E. Johnston. Although the Confederates enjoyed early success, routing two Union divisions, the Union line was quickly reinforced. The events at Bentonville so damaged Johnston's forces, he surrendered to Sherman about a month later.

1895 CE – First Motion Picture Footage Taken

There is argument about who first invented the cinématographe, the first motion picture film camera, but the Lumière brothers, Auguste and Louis, made early and important advances in the new technology, such as the idea of perforating the edge of the film. On March 19, 1895, the Lumières used their new movie camera to record footage for the first time, showing workers leaving the Lumière factory. In December of the same year, they gave the first public screening at which admission was charged.

World's First Movie Poster

1918 CE – Time Zones and Daylight Savings Time Begin

When towns and villages were far apart and trade took days, each town or city operated on its own local solar time, measured by a sundial or other early time-telling instrument. In the United States, local town times made it almost impossible to compile accurate railroad timetables. Standardization was badly needed.

The first standard time came in navigation, because navigators needed accurate clocks and a standard time to calculate longitude. Official

Naval time was linked to the Royal Observatory in Greenwich, England, starting in 1847 and so Greenwich Mean Time because the first time zone. New Zealand came next, establishing New Zealand Mean Time in 1868.

In the United States, the idea of using four standard time zones was first proposed in 1870, and implemented by the railroads thirteen years later. The Standard Time Act of March 19, 1918, established U.S. time zones and rules for daylight savings time for the entire country.

Today, time zones are used worldwide, but each country makes its own rules.

1931 CE – Nevada Legalizes Gambling and Easy Divorce

The booming mining state of Nevada was filled with unregulated gambling, but in 1909, Nevada joined a growing nationwide trends and outlawed it. As the decline of mining and the Great Depression wreaked havoc with the economy, Nevada reconsidered, and on March 19, 1931, the governor signed into law both open gambling and the most liberal divorce laws in the country.

1932 CE – Sydney Harbour Bridge Opens

One of the iconic images of Sydney, Australia, the Sydney Harbour Bridge when it opened was the world's widest long-span bridge, and remains the fifth longest spanning arch-bridge and the tallest steel arch bridge in the world.

At the ribbon-cutting ceremony on opening day, Francis de Groot, member of a paramilitary group opposed to government policies, rode in on a horse, disguised as a cavalry officer, cut the ribbon with his sword and declared the bridge open. He was arrested and fined £5 after a psychiatric evaluation ruled he was sane.

Sydney Harbour Bridge

1943 CE – Suicide of Frank "The Enforcer" Nitti

Top lieutenant of Al Capone, gangster Frank Nitti became head of operations of the Chicago Outfit when Capone went to jail. Nitti and other top mobsters were indicted for extortion in 1943, and Nitti was set up to take the fall. Nitti, who was extremely claustrophobic, could not tolerate the idea of another jail term, and shot himself in the head with a pistol on March 19, 1943, the same day he was scheduled to go before the Grand Jury.

1945 CE – Attack on *USS Franklin*

The aircraft carrier *USS Franklin* had just launched a fighter attack force only 50 miles off the Japanese coast when they were attacked by a Japanese dive bomber.

Over 800 were killed and nearly 500 wounded, and the casualty count would have been much higher if not for the action of brave officers and crew, two of whom won the Medal of Honor for their actions.

Franklin, which survived and eventually returned to duty, was the most heavily damaged U.S. carrier to survive the war.

USS Franklin burning after attack, seen from *USS Santa Fe*, firefighting

1945 CE – Hitler Issues the "Nero Decree"

On March 19, 1945, Adolf Hitler issued the *Befehl betreffend Zerstörungsmaßnahmen im Reichsgebiet*, "Demolitions on Reich Territory Decree," ordering the destruction of German infrastructure to keep it from benefiting Allied armies moving into Germany. It was not carried out. The decree became known as the "Nero Decree" for the Roman emperor Nero, who was supposed to have engineered (and fiddled during) the Great Fire of Rome.

1954 CE – Willie Mosconi Sets a World Record

Legendary pool champion Willie Mosconi set a world record of running 526 consecutive balls without a miss during a straight pool exhibition in Springfield, Ohio. He began on March 19 and didn't finish until early the following morning, with 35 witnesses testifying to the feat.

1962 CE – Bob Dylan's First Album

Bob Dylan's (right) first album, titled simply *Bob Dylan*, was released by Columbia Records on March 19, 1962. The album, which only had two original Dylan songs, attracted little notice, mediocre reviews, and poor sales on first release. His second album, however, went platinum, effectively launching Dylan's career.

1979 CE – C-SPAN Goes Live

The Cable-Satellite Public Affairs Network, or C-SPAN was created by the cable industry to broadcast government proceedings and other public affairs. The first C-SPAN channel, providing gavel-to-gavel coverage of the U.S. House of Representatives, began broadcasting on March 19, 1979.

1981 CE – Falklands War Begins

On March 19, 1981, a group of Argentine scrap metal merchants and Argentine marines raised the Argentine flag on the Falklands (Malvinas) island of South Georgia in preparation for a military attack beginning a few weeks later. It took Britain some time to organize and send a fleet across the Atlantic, but by mid-June 1982, the Argentine forces were defeated and retired. Argentina continues to claim jurisdiction over the islands, but Britain has remained in control of them.

1987 CE – Jim Bakker Leaves *The PTL Club*

Evangelists Jim and Tammy Faye Bakker created and hosted *The PTL Club*, a Christian television program that began in 1974 and was carried on over 100 stations. They built the PTS Satellite Network and the theme park Heritage USA. Financial irregularities led to criminal charges being filed against Jim Bakker, and exposed his payments for the silence of Jessica Hahn, a church secretary who claimed to have been raped by Bakker and another minister. Bakker resigned the show on March 19, 1987. He was eventually found guilty of numerous charges and sentenced to 45 years, later reduced to eight.

1990 CE – Târgu Mureş Conflict

Ethnic Hungarians and Romanians in the Transylvanian city of Târgu Mureş began a series of violent clashes beginning on March 19, 1990, that left a number of dead and several hundred injured. Romanian television broadcast the riots nationally, and media around the world covered the event. The exact causes and triggers of the riots remains unclear.

2011 CE – Libyan Intervention

On March 19, 2011, a NATO coalition including French, British, Canadian, and American forces began air attacks on Libya to aid rebels in ending the regime of Muammar Gaddafi (معمر محمد أبو منيار القذافي). Active intervention ended with Gadafi's death on October 20, 2011.

Who Was Born
on March 19?

Adventure

Wyatt Earp (March 19, 1848 — January 13, 1929)

Western law enforcer Wyatt Earp (photo next page) worked in Wichita and Dodge City, Kansas and also in Tombstone, Arizona. He fought in the Gunfight at the O.K. Corral; earning him the reputation of the "toughest and deadliest [Old West] gunman of his day."

Sir Richard Francis Burton (March 19, 1821 — October 20, 1980)

Legendary British adventurer and explorer Sir Richard Francis Burton (not the actor) spoke 29 languages, translated *One Thousand and One Nights (The Arabian Nights)* into English, visited Mecca in disguise, and was the first European to see Lake Tanganyika. He wrote books about human behavior, travel, falconry, sexual customs (he arranged the first English publication of the *Kama Sutra*), fencing, and many other topics.

The Dodge City Peace Commission, June 1883. Standing (left to right), W. H. Harris, Luke Short, Bat Masterson. Sitting (l-r), Charlie Bassett, **Wyatt Earp,** Frank McLain, Neil Brown

David Livingstone (March 19, 1813 — May 1, 1873)

Scotsman David Livingstone was a medical missionary and explorer in Africa. A national hero in Britain, he was a scientist, an anti-slavery crusader, and an important European explorer of the African continent.

Late in life, he lost contact with the outside world, and the New York *Herald* newspaper sent exploring journalist Henry Morton Stanley to find him.

Stanley discovered Livingston on the shores of Lake Tanganyika and greeted him by saying, "Dr. Livingtone, I presume?" a phrase that has gone down in history. (Livingstone's reply was, "Yes. I feel thankful that I am here to welcome you.")

The meeting of Stanley and Livingstone

Arts

Gualtiero Marchesi (March 19, 1930 —)

Award-winning chef Marchesi was the first celebrity chef to design two hamburgers and a dessert for McDonalds. He has won a number of top awards in gastronomy and was the international president of Euro-Toques, an association of the world's most important chefs.

Benito Jacovitti (March 19, 1923 — December 3, 1997)

Jacovitti was one of the most prolific and best-known comic book artists in Italy. His well-known characters include cowboy Cocco Bill and private eye Tom Ficcanaso.

Josef Albers (March 19, 1888 — March 25, 1976)

Influential German-American artist and educator Josef Albers specialized in geometric abstraction. He is best known for his series *Homage to the Square*; paintings in the series have sold for more than $1.5 million. His murals and other work are in such notable buildings as the Pan Am Building, the Corning Glass Building, the Rochester Institute of Technology, and others.

Charles Marion Russell (March 19, 1864 — October 24, 1926)

Charlie "Kid" Russell created more than 2,000 paintings and sculptures chronicling the American Old West. His 1918 painting *Piegans* sold for $5.6 million in 2005. The C. M. Russell Museum Complex in Montana holds his collection.

"The Herd Quitter," by Charles Marion Russell

Alonzo Cano (March 19, 1601 — September 3, 1667)

Spanish painter and sculptor Alonzo Cano was Royal Architect and Court Painter to King Philip IV. In a fit of temper, he broke a statue of a saint, a capital offense. He was tortured, but released back into the King's service.

Georges de La Tour (March 19, 1593 — January 30, 1652)

French Baroque painter de La Tour mostly painted religions chiaroscuro scenes. His work was forgotten for many years but was rediscovered in 1915. He was an influence on the 1982 film *The Draughtsman's Contract*, and one of his paintings is in Ariel's grotto in the Disney film *The Little Mermaid*.

"The Fortune Teller," Georges de La Tour

Business and Technology

Eduardo Saverin (March 19, 1982 —)

Brazilian internet entrepreneur Eduardo Saverin is one of the five co-founders of Facebook, with a net worth estimated at $2 billion.

Film, TV and Theater

Craig Lamar Taylor (March 19, 1989 —)

Taylor had a supporting role as the title character's friend in the TV series *Malcolm in the Middle* from 2000 to 2005.

Josie Loren (March 19, 1987 —)

Loren played Kaylie on *Make It or Break It*, and also appeared in the film *17 Again*.

Rachel Blanchard (March 19, 1976 —)

Blanchard played Cher in the TV series *Clueless* and Sally on *Flight of the Conchords*.

Connor Trinneer (March 19, 1969 —)

Trinneer played Trip Tucker on *Star Trek: Enterprise* and Michael on *Stargate Atlantis*.

Jake Weber (March 19, 1964 —)

Weber had major roles in *Dawn of the Dead* and *Meet Joe Black*, and played the husband of psychic Allison DuBois in the TV series *Medium*.

Mary Scheer (March 19, 1963 —)

Scheer was in the original cast of *MADtv*, played Freddie's mother on *iCarly*, and was Alice the zookeeper in *The Penguins of Madagascar*.

Fred Stoller (March 19, 1958 —)

Stoller had recurring roles on *Everybody Loves Raymond* and *Ned's Declassified School Survival Guide*. He wrote two episodes of *Seinfeld*, including the classic "The Soup."

Bruce Willis (March 19, 1955 —)

Bruce Willis first became known as the co-star of the TV series *Moonlighting*, and went on to star in the *Die Hard* series, *Pulp Fiction*, *The Fifth Element*, and many other movies.

Harvey Weinstein (March 19, 1952 —)

Producer Harvey Weinstein co-founded Miramax Films and The Weinstein Company. He won an Academy Award for producing *Shakespeare in Love*, and has also won seven Tony Awards. Miramax hits have included *Sex, Lies, and Videotape, The Crying Game, The English Patient,* and *Good Will Hunting*.

Glenn Close (March 19, 1947 —)

Glenn Close was nominated for three Academy Awards for her first three film roles in *The World According to Garp, The Big Chill*, and *The Natural*, and received additional nominations for *Fatal Attraction, Dangerous Liaisons*, and *Albert Nobbs*. She has also won three Tonys, an Obie, three Emmys, two Golden Globes, and a Screen Actor's Guild Award.

Ursula Andress (March 19, 1936 —)

Actress and sex symbol Ursula Andress (left) became the first Bond girl for her role in 1962's *Dr. No* (right), and went on to play opposite Elvis Presley in *Fun in Acapulco*, Frank Sinatra and Dean Martin in *4 for Texas*, and Marcello Mastroianni in *The 10ᵗʰ Victim*. She was named one of the "100 Sexiest Stars in Film History."

Burt Metcalfe (March 19, 1935 —)

Metcalfe was the only producer of the TV series M*A*S*H to stay with the series for its entire run. He received 13 Primetime Emmy Award nominations.

Nancy Malone (March 19, 1935 —)

Malone had featured roles in TV series including *Naked City, Guiding Light*, and *The Long Hot Summer*. She later became the first female vice-president of television at 20th Century Fox and won an Emmy for producing *Bob Hope: The First 90 Years*.

Richard Williams (March 19, 1933 —)

Richard Williams won two Academy Awards as animation director for *Who Framed Roger Rabbit* and designed the title sequences for *What's New, Pussycat?* and two *Pink Panther* films.

Renée Taylor (March 19, 1933 —)

Taylor received an Academy Award nomination for co-writing *Lovers and Other Strangers* with her husband Joseph Bologna, but is best known for playing the mother of Fran Drescher's character in the TV sitcom *The Nanny*.

Phyllis Newman (March 19, 1933 —)

Newman won the Tony for Best Featured Actress in a Musical for her role in *Subways Are For Sleeping*, and also played Rene Buchanan on *One Life to Live*. She was popular as a game show panelist and talk show guest in the 1960s and 1970s. She founded the Phyllis Newman Women's Health Initiative f and received a special Tony for her humanitarian work.

Patrick McGoohan (March 19, 1928 — January 13, 2009)

McGoohan's first major role was in the 1960s British TV series *Danger Man*, (U.S.: *Secret Agent*). He co-created the cult classic TV series *The Prisoner*. He won two Emmys for his work on *Columbo* and appeared in movies including *Ice Station Zebra* and *Silver Streak*.

Giuseppe Rotunno (March 19, 1923 —)

Italian cinematographer Rotunno won seven Silver Ribbon awards and received an Academy Award nomination for *All That Jazz*.

Pamela Britton (March 19, 1923 — July 17, 1974)

Britton played Lorelei in TV's *My Favorite Martian*, and also starred in the 1950 film noir *D.O.A.*.

Tommy Cooper (March 19, 1921 — April 15, 1984)

British comic magician Tommy Cooper was known for his trademark red fez. He died of a heart attack while appearing on live television in 1984's Live From Her Majesty's. Because his act often involved magic tricks appearing to go wrong, there was initial uncertainty about whether the heart attack was real.

Tige Andrews (March 19, 1920 — January 27, 2007)

Andrews played Captain Greer on *The Mod Squad* and was a Klingon in the original *Star Trek* series.

Peggy Ahern (March 19, 1917 — October 24, 2012)

Ahern appeared in eight of the *Our Gang/Little Rascals* film comedies.

Eric Christmas (March 19, 1916 — July 22, 2000)

British actor Christmas was known as the high school principal in the *Porky's* comedy films and as Reverend Diddymore in the sitcom *Amen*. He also appeared in *Harold and Maude, The Philadelphia Story,* and *Bugsy*.

Patricia Morison (March 19, 1914 or 1915 —)

Morison had small parts as the "other woman" in such films as *Lady on a Train, Song of the Thin Man,* and *Tarzan and the Huntress*, but went on to Broadway stardom as the lead in the original stage production of *Kiss Me, Kate*.

Fred Clark (March 19, 1914 — December 5, 1968)

Fred Clark appeared in such films as *Sunset Boulevard, How to Marry a Millionaire, Daddy Longlegs*, and *Auntie Mame*. He played neighbor Harry Morton on the *Burns and Allen* TV series.

Louis Hayward (March 19, 1909— February 21, 1985)

British actor Louis Hayward played the title role in *The Saint in New York*, both title roles in *The Man in the Iron Mask*, and won both a Bronze Star and a Best Documentary Oscar for filming the World War II Battle of Tarawa.

Joseph Mielziner (March 19, 1901 — March 15, 1976)

Mielziner, known as "the most successful set designer of the Golden era of Broadway," won five Tony awards out of twelve nominations, designing scenery and lighting for over 200 shows, including *South Pacific, Guys and Dolls, The King and I,* and *Gypsy.* He won an Oscar for for art directing the 1955 film *Picnic.*

Jackie "Moms" Mabley (March 19, 1894 — May 23, 1975)

One of the most successful entertainers on the "chitlin' circuit" of African-American vaudeville, "Moms" Mabley recorded over 20 comedy albums, appeared in movies, famously played Carnegie Hall, and appeared in numerous episodes of The Smothers Brothers Comedy Hour.

Billed as "The Funniest Woman in the World," Mabley's edgy and often X-rated humor covered racism, sexism, and other taboo topics. She came out as a lesbian at the age of 27, though her comic persona focused on her interested in handsome young men.

She was the oldest person to ever have a U.S. Top 40 hit with a satirical cover of "Abraham, Martin, and John" in 1969.

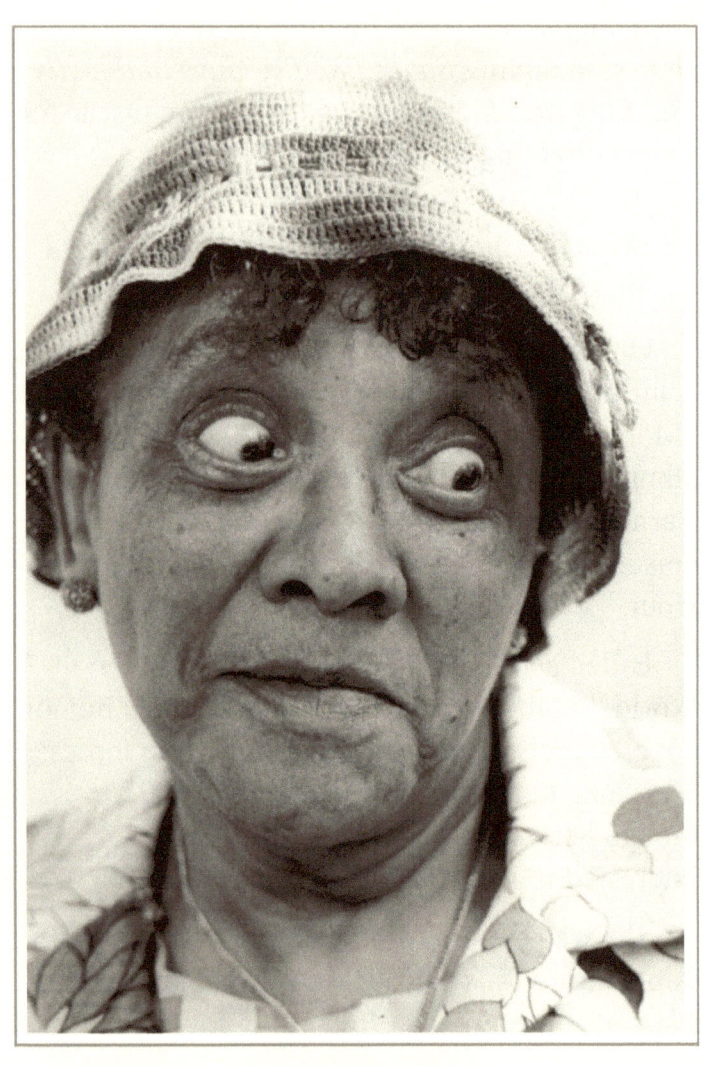

Jackie "Moms" Mabley

Military

Robert C. Cole (March 19, 1915 — September 18, 1944)

Lieutenant Colonel Robert Cole parachuted into Normandy on D-Day, and won the Medal of Honor by leading "Cole's Charge," a bayonet charge against dug-in German troops.

Joseph Carroll (March 19, 1910— January 20, 1991)

USAF General Joseph Carroll was founding director of the Defense Intelligence Agency (DIA) and the Air Force Office of Special Investigations.

Adolf Eichmann (March 19, 1906— May 31, 1962)

Adolf Eichman was one of the primary organizers and managers of the Holocaust, arranging mass deportation of Jews to ghettos and extermination camps. He fled to Argentina after the war and was captured by Israeli Mossad operatives. He was convicted in an Israeli court of crimes against humanity and other war crimes, and hanged in 1962, the only person executed in Israel by decision of a civilian court.

James Van Fleet (March 19, 1892 — September 23, 1992)

U.S. General James Van Fleet commanded United Nations forces during the end of the Korean War and implemented the Truman Doctrine in Greece. President Harry S. Truman said of him, "General Van Fleet was the best general we have ever had."

Joseph Stilwell (March 19, 1883 — October 12, 1946)

U.S. Army four-star General Joseph "Vinegar Joe" Stilwell was the senior military officer for the China-Burma-India Theater of World War II and served chief of staff to Chinese Generalissimo Chiang Kai-Shek. Deprived of resources that went to the European and Pacific theaters, Stilwell was known for his innovative and creative tactics, but continually clashed with Chinese and British leadership, leading to his removal and replacement in 1944.

Alfred von Tirpitz (March 19, 1849 — March 6, 1930)

Imperial German Navy Grand Admiral Alfred von Tirpitz rebuilt the German Imperial Navy and fought the British Navy to a draw at the Battle of Jutland.

Grand Admiral Alfred von Tirpitz

Music

Ricky Wilson (March 19, 1953 — October 12, 1985)

Wilson was a founding member and the original guitarist of the B-52s.

Ruth Pointer (March 19, 1946 —)

Pointer is the eldest member of the R&B/disco group The Pointer Sisters.

Paul Atkinson (March 19, 1946 — April 1, 2004)

Atkinson played guitar for The Zombies, and in later life became a recording executive who discovered and signed ABBA, Judas Priest, and Mr. Mister.

Clarence "Frogman" Henry (March 19, 1937 —)

R&B singer and pianist Henry's hits include 1956's "Ain't Got No Home" and 1961's "(I Don't Know Why) But I Do" and "You Always Hurt the One You Love." He opened eighteen concerts for The Beatles on their 1964 U.S. tour. He is in the Rockabilly Hall of Fame and the Louisiana Music Hall of Fame.

Ornette Coleman (March 19, 1930 —)

Saxophonist Ornette Coleman is best known as one of the innovators of the free jazz movement, and won the 2007 Pulitzer Prize for Music for his album *Sound Grammar*.

Ornette Coleman

Francesco Gasparini (March 19, 1661 — February 22, 1727)

Italian composer Gasparini wrote the first opera using the story of Hamlet, though not Shakespeare's version. His operas continue to be performed in Europe.

Politics and Law

Fayez Banihammad (فايز راشد احمد حسن القاضي بني حمد) (March 19, 1977 — September 11, 2001)

Banihammad was one of the September 11, 2001 hijackers, aboard United Airlines Flight 175 that flew into the South Tower of the World Trade Center.

Yegor Gaidar (Егор Гайда́р) (March 19, 1956 — December 16, 2009)

As Acting Prime Minister of Russia, Gaidar pushed through controversial shock therapy reforms in the wake of the dissolution of the Soviet Union, and is credited by many economists for saving Russia from complete collapse.

Sirhan Sirhan (سرحان بشارة سرحان)
(March 19, 1944 —)

Sirhan Bishara Sirhan, a Palestinian Christian of Jordanian citizenship, assassinated presidential candidate Senator Robert F. Kennedy on June 5, 1968. He was sentenced to death, later commuted to life in prison.

Egon Krenz (March 19, 1937 —)

Krenz was the last head of state of East Germany before reunification.

Brent Scowcroft (March 19, 1925 —)

USAF Lieutenant General Brent Scowcroft was National Security Advisor to Presidents Gerald Ford and George H. W. Bush.

Albert Speer (March 19, 1905— September 1, 1981)

German architect Albert Speer was Minister of Armaments and War Production for the Third Reich. He was one of the only senior Nazi officials who accepted moral responsibility for his involvement in Nazi war crimes, and served 20 years in prison. After his release, he wrote two bestselling books, *Inside the Third Reich* and *Spandau: The Secret Diaries.*

John Sirica (March 19, 1904 — August 14, 1992)

U. S. District Court Chief Judge John "Maximum John" Sirica presided over the trial of the Watergate burglars and ordered President Richard Nixon to turn over his White House recordings. He was named *Time* magazine's Man of the Year in 1973.

Earl Warren (March 19, 1891 — July 9, 1974)

Former California governor Earl Warren (left) was the 14th Chief Justice of the U.S. Supreme Court. Landmark decisions of the Warren Court including Brown v. Board of Education (school desegregation), Miranda v. Arizona (requiring the "Miranda warning"), Engel v. Vitale (banning mandatory school prayer), and Griswold v. Connecticut (establishing the Constitutional right to privacy). He also chaired the Warren Commission that investigated the assassination of John F. Kennedy.

Edith Nourse Rogers (March 19, 1881 — September 10, 1960)

First woman elected to Congress from Massachusetts, Edith Nourse Rogers helped draft and sponsor the G.I. Bill and legislation to create the Women's Army Corps (WAC).

William Jennings Bryan (March 19, 1860 — July 26, 1925)

American politician William Jennings Bryan, known as "the Great Commoner," ran three times for U.S. President (poster next page), promoted Free Silver coinage (he made the famous "Cross of Gold" speech denouncing the gold standard), and represented the anti-evolution side in the famous Scopes Trial of 1925.

Túpac Amaru II (March 19, 1742 — May 18, 1781)

In 1780, Túpac Amaru II led an unsuccessful indigenous uprising against Spanish rule in Peru. He was killed by torture and his family was executed in front of him before he died. After his death, he became a semi-mythical hero in the cause of Peruvian independence and native rights.

Campaign poster from William Jennings Bryan's 1900
campaign for U.S. President

Thomas McKean (March 19, 1734 — June 24, 1817)

Thomas McKean signed the Declaration of Independence and the Articles of Confederation at the birth of the United States. He was the second elected President of the United States in Congress Assembled under the Articles of Confederation.

William Bradford (March 19, 1590 — May 9, 1657)

Bradford was governor of the Plymouth Colony in Massachusetts for over 30 years. He was the first public official in the United States to designate Thanksgiving Day. His journals were published as *Of Plymouth Plantation*.

Religion

Hans Küng (March 19, 1928 —)

Catholic priest Hans Küng was forbidden to teach theology by the Vatican for his public rejection of the doctrine of papal infallibility. He has received numerous awards including the Karl Barth Prize, the Otto Hahn Peace Medal, and the International Council of Christianity and Judaism's Interfaith Gold Medallion.

José de Anchieta (March 19, 1534 — June 9, 1597)

Jesuit missionary to Brazil, de Anchieta helped found São Paulo and Rio de Janeiro, led the conversion of native Brazilians to Christianity, and as a poet became Brazil's first writer. He was beatified in 1980.

Science and Medicine

Mario J. Molina (March 19, 1943 —)

Molina shared the 1995 Nobel Prize in Chemistry for his work on the threat of CFCs on the ozone layer. He was the first Mexican-born citizen to receive the award.

Henry Morgentaler (March 19, 1923 —)

Canadian physician Morgentaler defied anti-abortion laws in Canada, and won important judicial battles that legalized abortion in that country. He received the Order of Canada.

Leonidas Alaoglu (March 19, 1914— August 1981)

Canadian-American mathematician Alaoglu is best known for his work in topology, including the Banach-Alaoglu and the Bourbaki-Alaoglu theorems. The Leonidus Alaoglu Memorial Lectures at Caltech are named in his honor.

Frédéric Joliot-Curie (March 19, 1900—August 14, 1958)

Frédéric Joliot-Curie shared the 1935 Nobel Prize in Chemistry with his wife Irène Joliot-Curie, daughter of famed scientists Marie Skłodowska-Curie and Pierre Curie, for their discovery of artificial radioactivity. He was active in the French Resistance in World War II, using his chemistry background to manufacture Molotov cocktails.

Frédéric and Irène Joliot-Curie

Sir Normal Haworth (March 19, 1883 — March 19, 1950)

Haworth shared the 1939 Nobel Prize in Chemistry for synthesizing Vitamin C and analyzing the structure of carbohydrates. His method for rendering the 3-D structure of complex sugars, known as the Haworth projection, continues to be widely used. The day of his birth and his death are the same: March 19.

Jean Astruc (March 19, 1684 — May 5, 1766)

Professor of Medicine Jean Astruc wrote the first major work on syphilis and venereal diseases. He also wrote textual analysis of works of scripture, and was the first to advance the "documentary hypothesis" about the Book of Genesis.

Sports and Games

Clayton Kershaw (March 19, 1988 —)

Los Angeles Dodgers pitcher Kershaw won the Pitching Triple Crown and the Cy Young Award in 2011, and the Roberto Clemente Award for humanitarian service in 2012.

Joe Kapp (March 19, 1938 —)

Joe Kapp is only player to have quarterbacked in the Superbowl, the Rose Bowl, and the Grey Cup. He is in the Canadian Football Hall of Fame and the College Football Hall of Fame.

Gay Brewer (March 19, 1932 — August 31, 2007)

Golfer Brewer won the 1949 Junior Amateur and the 1967 Master's.

Eugene Selznick (March 19, 1930 — June 10, 2012)

Eugene Selznick captained the U.S. men's national volleyball team for 17 years and two gold medals, and coached the U.S. women's volleyball team to a gold medal. He was inducted into the Volleyball Hall of Fame and the International Jewish Sports Hall of Fame.

Richie Ashburn (March 19, 1927 — September 9, 1997)

Known variously as "Putt-Putt," "The Tilden Flash," and "Whitey," baseball outfielder Richie Ashburn is best known for his eleven-year career with the Philadelphia Phillies. He was inducted into the National Baseball Hall of Fame in 1995.

Joe Gaetjens (March 19, 1924 — presumed dead July 10, 1964)

Haitian soccer player Gaetjens scored the winning goal for the United States team in the 1950 FIFA World Cup in a 1-0 upset of favorite England.

He was arrested in his home country by the Tonton Macoutes secret police and never seen again. He was named to the U.S. National Soccer Hall of Fame in 1976.

László Szabó (March 19, 1917 — August 8, 1998)

Hungarian chess grandmaster Szabó was one of the top players in the world, representing his country in 11 Chess Olympiads.

Jay Berwanger (March 19, 1914 — June 26, 2002)

Halfback Jay Berwanger won the first Downtown Athletic Club Trophy (later renamed the Heisman Trophy), and was the first player drafted by the NFL, but the Philadelphia Eagles couldn't handle his salary demands of $1,000 per game. He is a member of the College Football Hall of Fame.

Joe Rollino (March 19, 1905 or 1916 — January 11, 2010)

Weightlifter and strongman "Mighty" Joe Rollino was known as the "world's strongest man" in the 1920s for lifting 3,200 pounds with his back, 635 pounds with a single finger, and 450 pounds with his teeth. He also boxed under the ring name of "Kid Dundee."

He served in the Pacific during World War II, receiving a Silver Star, a Bronze Star, and three Purple Hearts. In one remarkable battle, Rollino "ran onto the field, grabbed two men under one arm, two under another, and brought them back behind the lines. And he did this several times."

In later life, Rollino worked as a longshoreman and as Greta Garbo's bodyguard. Records of the year of his birth differ. At the age of 103 (or 92), he could still bend quarters with his teeth. On January 11, 2010, he was hit by a car and died at the age of either 93 or 104.

Writing

Jill Abramson (March 19, 1954 —)

In 2011, journalist and editor Jill Abramson became the first female executive editor of the New York *Times*.

Philip Roth (March 19, 1933 —)

Roth won the National Book Award for his 1959 novella *Goodbye, Columbus* and a Pulitzer Prize for 1997's *American Pastoral.* He was also known for his controversial 1969 best-selling *Portnoy's Complaint.*

Irving Wallace (March 19, 1916 — June 29, 1990)

Irving Wallace's numerous best-selling novels included *The Prize, The Man,* and *The Word*, and nonfiction including *The People's Almanac* and *The Book of Lists.*

William Allingham (March 19, 1824 — November 18, 1889)

William Allingham is best known for his poem "The Faeries." His poetry has been quoted in the movie *Willy Wonka and the Chocolate Factory* and *Don't Look in the Basement*, as well as in comics and science fiction.

Tobias Smollett (March 19, 1721 — September 17, 1771)

Scottish author Smollett wrote humorous, anecdotal novels with titles like *The Adventures of Roderick Random* or *Peregrine Pickle.* He influenced later novelists including Charles Dickens.

Who Died on March 19?

Arts and Design

Willem de Kooning (April 24, 1904 — March 19, 1997)

De Kooning was part of the New York School of abstract expressionists.

Garry Winogrand (January 14, 1928 — March 19, 1984)

Street photographer Garry Winogrand chronicled American life in the early 1960s.

Anne Klein (August 3, 1923 — March 19, 1974)

Fashion designer Anne Klein developed a brand of sportswear and other clothing.

Vasily Surikov (Василий Су́риков) (January 24 [O.S. January 12], 1848 — March 19 [O.S. March 6], 1916)

Surikov was a well-known Russian painter of historical subjects, some of whose paintings are among the best known paintings in Russia.

Detail from "Morning of the Execution of Streltsy"
by Vasily Surikov

Business

John DeLorean (January 6, 1925 — March 19, 2005)

Automobile engineer and executive DeLorean developed the Pontiac GTO and Firebird for GM, then began DeLorean Motor Company, famous for the DeLorean DMC-12, featured in *Back to the Future* and its sequels. He was arrested in 1982 for drug trafficking, but was acquitted on the grounds of entrapment.

Film, TV and Theater

Paul Scofield (January 21, 1922 — March 19, 2008)

Scofield won the Academy Award for his role as Sir Thomas Moore in 1996's *A Man for All Seasons*.

Calvert DeForest (July 23, 1921 — March 19, 2007)

DeForest played Larry "Bud" Melman on *Late Night With David Letterman*.

Émile Genest (July 27, 1921 — March 19, 2003)

Canadian actor Genest began in the French radio and television series The Plouffe Family, and played the lead in the film *The Incredible Journey*.

Cesare Danova (March 1, 1926 — March 19, 1992)

Danova played Elvis Presley's rival Count Elmo Mancini in *Viva Las Vegas*, a Mafia don in Martin Scorcese's *Mean Streets*, and the mayor in *National Lampoon's Animal House*.

Richard Beckinsale (July 6, 1947 — March 19, 1979)

English actor Beckinsale played BBC sitcom characters Lennie in *Porridge* and Alan in *Rising Damp*. He is the father of actresses Samantha and Kate Beckinsale.

Edward Platt (February 14, 1916 — March 19, 1974)

Platt is best known for playing the Chief in the TV sitcom *Get Smart*.

Military and Exploration

Clancy Lyall (October 25, 1925 — March 19, 2012)

Lyall served during World War II with Easy Company, chronicled in the book and miniseries *Band of Brothers*. He later served in the Korean War and in Indochina, winning three Purple Hearts and two Bronze Stars.

Admiral Sir James Somerville (July 17, 1882 — March 19, 1949)

Somerville was one of the most famous British admirals of World War II, serving in the Mediterranean Sea and the Indian Ocean.

John Campbell, 1st Earl of Breadalbane and Holland (1636 — March 19, 1717)

Scottish nobleman "Slippery John " Campbell was implicated in the Massacre of Glencoe. An extremely influential and rich man, he reputedly owned the best wig in Scotland. He took money to send 1,200 men to the Jacobite uprising of 1715, but only sent 300.

Robert de La Salle (November 21, 1643 — March 19, 1687)

René-Robert Cavelier, Sieur de La Salle, explored the Great Lakes region for France, claiming the entire Mississippi River basin for his country.

Music

Luther Ingram (November 30, 1937 — March 19, 2007)

Ingram's 1972 R&B hit "(If Loving You Is Wrong) I Don't Want to be Right" reached #3 on the Hot 100. He co-authored "Respect Yourself" for the Staples Singers and was an opening act for Isaac Hayes.

Charles-Louis Hanon (July 2, 1819 — March 19, 1900)

Hanon wrote *The Virtuoso Pianist in 60 Exercises*, the most widely used set of exercises in modern piano teaching.

Thomas Ken (July 1637 — March 19, 1711)

English Bishop Thomas Ken is known for "Praise God from whom all blessings flow," "Glory to Thee, my God, this night," and other hymns.

Politics and Law

William Hale Thompson (May 14, 1869 — March 19, 1944)

Republican Mayor of Chicago "Big Bill" Thompson (left) was described by the Chicago *Tribune*: "Thompson has meant filth, corruption, obscenity, idiocy and bankruptcy... He has given the city an international reputation for moronic buffoonery, barbaric crime, triumphant hoodlumism, unchecked graft, and a dejected citizenship... In his attempt to continue this he excelled himself as a liar and defamer of character."

Lloyd L. Gaines (1911 — disappeared March 19, 1939)

Gaines was the plaintiff in the 1938 case Gaines v. Canada, a landmark court case that held that a state providing schooling for white students was also required to provide in-state education to blacks as well. He left his Chicago fraternity house to buy stamps on March 19, 1939, and never returned.

Arthur Balfour (July 25, 1848 — March 19, 1930)

Prime Minister and later Foreign Secretary of the United Kingdom, Balfour (right) is known as the author of the Balfour Declaration of 1917, supporting the establishment of a Jewish homeland in Palestine.

John Bingham (January 21, 1815 — March 19, 1900)

Ohio congressman John Bingham was the principle framer of the Fourteenth Amendment to the Constitution and a prosecutor in the impeachment trial of President Andrew Johnson.

Science and Mathematics

Charles K. Johnson (July 24, 1924 — March 19, 2001)

President of the International Flat Earth Society, Johnson denied the round earth, the Apollo landings, and space exploration, on the grounds that they contradicted the Biblical teaching that the Earth was flat.

Louis de Broglie (August 15, 1892 — March 19, 1987)

French physicist Louis-Victor-Pierre-Raymond, 7th duc de Broglie, won the 1929 Nobel Prize in Physics for his work on wave-particle duality. The de Broglie wavelength shows that the wavelength of a subatomic particle is inversely proportional to its momentum.

Gaston Julia (February 3, 1893 — March 19, 1978)

French mathematician Gaston Julia developed the formula for the fractal known as the Julia set.

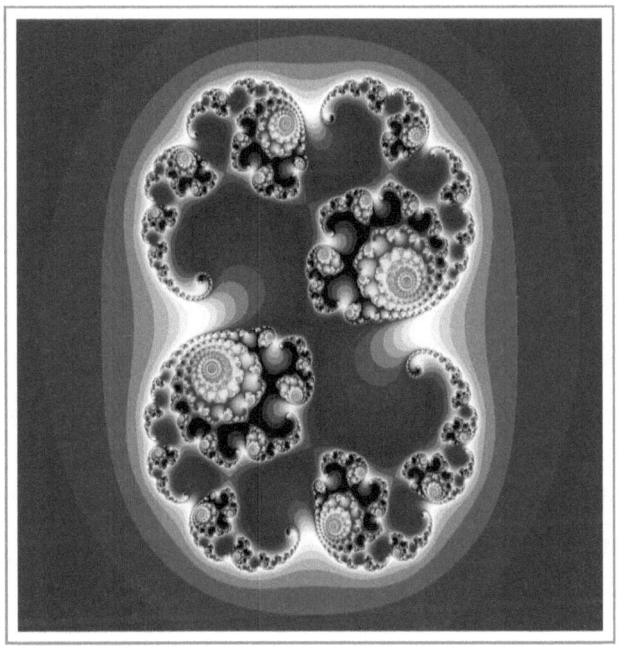

A Julia set fractal

Giuseppe Mercalli (May 21, 1850 — March 19, 1914)

Mercalli developed the original Mercalli scale for measuring earthquakes. As modified by subsequent scientists, it is still in use today.

William Karl Ritter von Haidinger
(February 5, 1795 — March 19, 1871)

A multidisciplinary scientist, Haidinger was the first to identify and describe Haidinger's brush, showing that the human eye can perceive polarization of light.

Sports

Joanne Weaver (December 19, 1935 — March 19, 2000)

Right fielder "Joltin' Jo" Weaver played in the All-American Girls Professional Baseball League in the early 1950s. She was named Player of the Year in 1984, and holds a single-season batting average of .429.

Bun Cook (September 18, 1904 — March 19, 1988)

Hockey Hall of Famer Bun Cook played for the New York Rangers, Boston Bruins, and Saskatoon Crescents from 1926 to 1937, and coached the Providence Reds and the Cleveland Barons to a record setting seven Calder Cup championships.

Writing

Arthur C. Clarke (December 16, 1917— March 19, 2008)

Arthur C. Clarke first proposed satellite communication from geosynchronous orbit, authored 2001: A Space Odyssey, discovered the underwater ruins of an ancient temple in Sri Lanka, and was considered one of the "Big Three" of science fiction along with Robert Heinlein and Isaac Asimov.

Edgar Rice Burroughs (September 1, 1875 — March 19, 1950)

American author Edgar Rice Burroughs is famed as the creator of *Tarzan of the Apes* (poster next page) and *John Carter of Mars*, among many other works.

Thomas Killigrew (February 7, 1612 — March 19, 1683)

English dramatist Thomas Killigrew was part of the court of King Charles II and played an important role in the revival of English drama after the Restoration.

Poster for the 1923 film *The Adventures of Tarzan*

Péter Pázmány (October 4, 1570 — March 19, 1637)

Catholic Cardinal Pázmány created the Hungarian literary language and is the author of the remarkable 1613 work *Guide to Truth*.

Ibn Khaldun (أبو زيد عبد الرحمن بن محمد بن خلدون الحضرمي) (May 27, 1332 — March 19, 1406)

Muslim historian Ibn Khaldun is considered one of the fathers of modern historiography, sociology, and economics, and as one of the greatest philosophers of the Muslim world. He is best known for his work *The Muqaddimah* (مقدّمة ابن خلدون).

March: The Third Month

Up from the sea, the wild north wind is blowing
Under the sky's gray arch;
Smiling I watch the shaken elm boughs, knowing
It is the wind of March.

— "March," John Greenleaf Whittier

In ancient Rome, March was the first month of the year. As the first month of spring, in the Mediterranean climate it marked the beginning of the military campaign season. That's why March (Martius) is named in honor of Mars, the Roman god of war.

Although the first month of the year was moved back to January sometime during the transition of Rome from a kingdom to a republic (historians differ), March was the first month of the year in Russia until the end of the 15th Century, and is the first month of the year in many other cultures and religions.

In the northern hemisphere, March 1 marks the beginning of meteorological spring. In the southern hemisphere, March is the equivalent of September, making southern hemisphere March the beginning of autumn.

March is one of the seven months that have 31 days in it. March starts on the same day of the week as November every year, and except for leap years starts on the same day as February. March starts on the same day of the week as the previous June except for leap years, and in leap years starts on the same day as the previous September and December.

March in Other Cultures

In Finland, March is called *maaliskuu* (earthy month). In Ukraine, it's *березень* (birch tree). Other names for March include *Lentmonat* (Saxon), *Hyld-monath* (Angles), and *sušec* (Slovene).

March Symbols

Birthstones: Aquamarine (right) and bloodstone, both representing courage.

Birth Flowers: Daffodils

Daffodils in Bagatelle Park, Paris, France

March Events

Honorary months: Presidents, Congresses, and nations around the world issue proclamations recognizing particular months to honor certain causes. These events generally fall in March. (All US unless otherwise noted.)

- National Nutrition Month
- American Red Cross Month
- Women's History Month (celebrated in Canada during October)

- Irish-American Heritage Month
- Colorectal Cancer Awareness Month
- Fire Prevention Month (The Philippines)

"March Madness": (United States) The NCAA Men's Division I Basketball Championship, popularly known as "March Madness" or the "Big Dance," is a single-elimination tournament to establish the champion college basketball team.

Multi-day events: Some March events span multiple days.

- **Nineteen Day Fast:** (Bahá'í Faith) March 2 through March 20

- **Multiple Sclerosis Awareness Week:** (U.S.) Sponsored by the National Multiple Sclerosis Society, MS Awareness Week is normally held on the second full week in March. The earliest it can begin is March 9 and the latest it can end is March 21.

Movable events: Some events change dates from year to year.

- **March Equinox:** As the Earth's axis tilts toward and away from the sun during the year, it reaches two extremes, known as the *solstices,* and two times in which the tilt is in the middle) neither toward nor away from the sun), known as the *equinoxes*. At the equinox, the length of the day and the length of the night are approximately equal.

The *vernal*, or spring, equinox is the official beginning of springtime. The *autumnal*, or fall, equinox is the official beginning of fall. The March Equinox, which falls between March 19 and March 21, depending on the year, is the *vernal equinox* (beginning of spring) in the Northern Hemisphere, and the *autumnal equinox* (beginning of fall) in the Southern Hemisphere.

- **Earth Day:** Earth Day, an international day to increase awareness and appreciation of our planet's natural environment, is held each year on the same day as the March equinox, between March 19 and March 21. The first Earth Day took place in 1970, and there are now Earth Day events held in over 140 nations around the world. Some communities celebrate Earth Week, which is the week containing Earth Day.

- **Nowruz:** New Year's Day in Iran is known as Nowruz, and it takes place on the same day as the March equinox, between March 19 and March 21. Nowruz is also a holiday in Turkey and some Central Asian countries, and is celebrated wherever large concentrations of Iranians live.

  It was originally a holiday of the Zoroastrian religion, and the Islamic rulers of Iran have attempted to suppress it, though with little success. Nowruz is also a holy day for Alawites, Alevis, and Bahá'í. Fire is the symbol of Nowruz, and large bonfires often play a part in festivities.

- **Passion Sunday:** The fifth Sunday of the Christian season of Lent is known as Passion Sunday in various Protestant denominations and by some traditionalist Catholics. Sometimes, the sixth Sunday of Lent is referred to as Passion Sunday, but it is more commonly known as Palm Sunday.

  Passion Sunday starts the two-week Passiontide, which ends on Holy Saturday, the day before Easter, commemorating the day that Jesus's body was laid in the tomb. The fifth Sunday of Lent can occur as early as March 8 (though the next time it will be that early is in 2285 CE), and as late as April 11.

- **Palm Sunday:** The moveable feast of Palm Sunday commemorates the triumphant entry of Jesus into Jerusalem, an event mentioned in all four gospels. In many Christian churches, palm leaves are distributed to the worshippers. The earliest date for Palm Sunday is March 15, and the latest is April 18.

- **Maundy Thursday:** The Thursday before Easter is Maundy Thursday, when the Last Supper took place. Because of its relation to Easter, the earliest day it can occur is March 19, and the latest it can occur is April 22.

March Zodiac Signs

From the perspective of someone on Earth, the Sun appears to move through the sky throughout the year, along a path astronomers call the ecliptic plane. The ecliptic plane is divided into twelve constellations, known as the zodiac, based on traditionally observed patterns of stars. On your birthday, you can't see your constellation, because it's part of the daytime sky.

The zodiac was first developed by Babylonian astronomers about 2,500 years ago. Because they were unaware that the Earth wobbles like a spinning top (a motion known as *precession*), they didn't make allowance for the fact that the Sun's path through the zodiac changes over time.

That means there are now two sets of dates for your birth sign. The tropical dates are the original Babylonian dates; the siderial dates tell you where the Sun actually appears as it moves along its annual path.

March 19 has the same astrological sign in both systems: Pisces.

Pisces

Tropical February 20 to March 20

Siderial March 15 to April 14

In the Roman legend of Venus and her son Cupid, they escaped the clutches of Typhon, known as the "father of all monsters," by transforming into fish and tying themselves together with rope. That's why the name Pisces is plural for fish. The constellation appears as a somewhat ragged "V" shape, representing the rope, with the "fish" located at the two rope ends.

In astrology, Pisces is a water sign, compatible with the other water signs Cancer and Scorpio, as well as with the earth signs Taurus, Virgo, and Capricorn. Pisceans are supposed to be imaginative, compassionate, unworldly, secretive, and escapist.

What Day of the Week is March 19?

On what day of the week does March 19 fall?

Surprisingly, this isn't an easy question. Because the calendar year is 365 days long (366 in leap years), it doesn't divide evenly by the seven days of the week.

Also, the Earth goes around the Sun in about 365-1/4 days, so a calendar tends to drift over time. That's why the same date falls on different weekdays in different years.

This is made even more complicated by a change in calendars that took place in 1582. Our modern calendar has its roots in ancient Rome, in a calendar reform conducted by Julius Caesar. Caesar commissioned mathematicians to attack the problem, and came up with the idea of *leap years,* and thus standardized the calendar for centuries to come. This was called the *Julian calendar.*

Over time, however, the small errors in Caesar's calculation compounded. That's why Pope Gregory XIII commissioned the *Gregorian calendar,* used in most of the world today. Some countries converted in 1582, when the calendar was first developed; some converted later; other still haven't changed.

Gregorian and Julian aren't the only types of calendars. The Hebrew year, the Islamic year, and many other calendars are used in different parts of the world and among different people.

You can convert Gregorian dates to other calendars, including the Hebrew calendar, the Islamic calendar, and even the Mayan calendar by visiting the Fourmilab Calendar Converter at http://www.fourmilab.ch/documents/calendar/.

A 50-year brass perpetual calendar.

Copyright, Credit, and Contact

Follow Us

Our blog Dobson's Improbable History features short articles on events and people associated with each day, and updates several times each week. Get the latest on Twitter @SidewiseThinker.

Contact Us

Find an error or a format problem? Want information about the series, about us, or about when the volume for your special day might be available? Please email us at editor@timespinnerpress.com.

Sources and Art Credits

All art and photographs are either in the public domain or used under a Creative Commons license. Attribution is provided where requested by the copyright owner or when of historical significance, listed below.

- The "Buy War Bonds" poster of a Tuskegee Airman is in the collection of the National Archives and Records Administration, and is in the public domain as an image created by the U.S. federal government.

- The photograph of Tuskegee Airman Capt. Andrew D. Turner is in the collection of the National Archives and Records Administration, and is in the public domain as an image created by the U.S. federal government.

- The 1985 poster advertising the Lumière brothers' production of *L'Arroseur arrosé* is in the public domain because its copyright has expired.

- The photograph of the Sydney Harbour Bridge was taken in 2011 by "Gnangarra," and is used here under the Creative Commons Attribution 2.5 Australia license, attribution: "Photographs by Gnangarra...commons.wikimedia.org."

- The official Navy photograph of the damaged *USS Franklin* is in the public domain as a work of the U.S. federal government.

- The cropped photograph of Bob Dylan is from a photograph of Dylan and Joan Baez at the 1963 March on Washington, and was taken by Rowland Scherman for the U.S. Information Agency. It is now in the collection of the National Archives and

Records Service. It is in the public domain as a work of the U.S. federal government.

- The 1883 photograph of the Dodge City Peace Commission is in the public domain because its copyright has expired.

- The illustration of the meeting of Stanley and Livingstone is from an 1876 edition of Henry Stanley's book *How I Found Livingstone*. It is in the public domain because its copyright has expired.

- The painting "The Herd Quitter" by C. M. Russell is in the public domain because its copyright has expired. The original painting is in the Montana Historical Society MacKay Collection, Helena, Montana.

- The painting "The Fortune Teller" by Georges de La Tour is in the public domain because its copyright has expired. The original painting is in the collection of the Metropolitan Museum of Art.

- The publicity photograph of Ursula Andress from the movie *Dr. No* is in the public domain because it was published in the U.S. between 1923 and 1977 without a copyright notice.

- The publicity photograph of "Moms" Mabley from the television series *The Smothers Brothers Comedy Hour* is in the public domain because it was published in the U.S. between 1923 and 1977 without a copyright notice.

- The photograph of Alfred von Tirpitz is in the public domain because its copyright has expired.

- The 1994 photograph of Ornette Coleman was taken by Geert Vandepole and is used here under the Creative Commons Attribution-Share Alike 2.0 Generic license.

- The photograph of Chief Justice Earl Warren was taken by the Harris & Ewing photography firm. Their works were all donated to the Library of Congress Prints and Photographs Division, and have been released into the public domain.

- The poster from the 1900 presidential campaign of William Jennings Bryan is in the public domain because its copyright has expired.

- No known copyright restrictions exist on the photograph of Frédéric and Irène Joliot-Curie by James Lebenthal.

- The 1881 painting "Morning of the Execution of Streltsy" by Vasily Surikov is in the public domain because its copyright has expired. The original can be found in the Tretyakov Gallery, Moscow.

- The photograph of Chicago mayor William Hale Thompson was taken by the Harris & Ewing photography firm. Their works were all donated to the Library of Congress Prints and Photographs Division, and have been released into the public domain.

- The photograph of Prime Minister Arthur Balfour was taken by George Grantham Bain. It is in the public domain because its first publication occurred prior to 1923. The photograph is in the Library of Congress Prints and Photographs Division.

- The photograph of a Julia set fractal is by Solkoll, and has been released into the public domain by its author.

- The 1921 poster for *The Adventures of Tarzan*, starring Elmo Lincoln, is in the public domain because its copyright has expired. The image is in the collection of the Library of Congress Prints and Photographs Division.

- The illustration of the month of March used on the back cover and in the interior is from the French Gothic illuminated manuscript *Les Très Riches Heures du duc de Berry* by the Limbourg Brothers, Jean Colombe, and an intermediate painter whose name is lost to history. It is in the public domain because its copyright has expired.

- The photograph of aquamarine has been released into the public domain.

- The photograph of daffodils is by Myrabella, and is licensed under the Creative Commons Attribution-Share Alike 3.0 Unported license.

- The 1917 Women's Suffrage demonstration comes from the Library of Congress, Prints and Photographs Division, LC-USZ62-31799 DLC, and is in the public domain because its copyright has expired.

- The 50-year perpetual calendar photograph is in the public domain.

The month of March, from the illuminated manuscript *Les Très Riches Heures du duc de Berry*

www.ingramcontent.com/pod-product-compliance
Lightning Source LLC
Chambersburg PA
CBHW050422290526
45786CB00003B/1369